Three Wishes

Written by Polly Peterson
Illustrated by Arieh Zeldich

Once upon a time, a man went out to
cut some wood for his fire. He saw an old
tree that he had never seen before.

"What a funny old tree," he said. "How
could I have missed seeing it all these years?"

He started to chop down the old tree.
But just as he started to chop, a voice
called out. "Do not chop me!" it said.
Who could be talking?

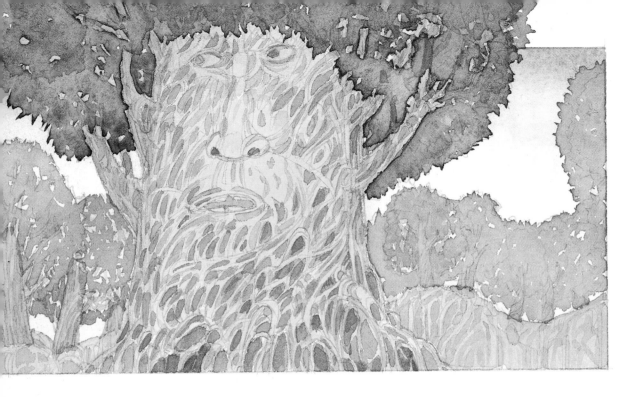

"If you stop, I will give you three
wishes," said the voice.

The man thought he must be dreaming.
Could the tree be talking?

The man put down his ax.

The tree said, "Go back to your house. Tell your wife about the three wishes. Then whatever you wish for, you will have."

The man could not believe his good
luck. He picked up his ax and walked home
— just as fast as he could go!

As he walked, he thought about what he could wish for. Should he wish for gold coins? What would it be like to have all the riches in the world?

Should he wish for a big house? Maybe
he should wish for two houses. Then he
could have one house in the forest and one
by the sea.

When the man got home, his wife was cooking soup.

"Did you bring home some wood for the fire?" she asked.

"No, but you'll never believe it," the man said. "I have something much better."

He told his wife about the tree and the three wishes.

"Well, I don't believe it," said his wife.
"You must have been dreaming. But now that
you're home, we might as well eat."

She put a small pot of soup on the
table. "All we have is this small pot of
soup," she said. "How I wish we had some
nice big eggs!"

In the wink of an eye, some nice big
eggs lay on the table!

"Oh, no!" shouted the man. "Now see what you've done. You've wished for some eggs! What a silly thing to do! I wish those eggs were stuck to your ears."

And in the wink of an eye — Oh, no!
Those eggs were stuck to her ears!

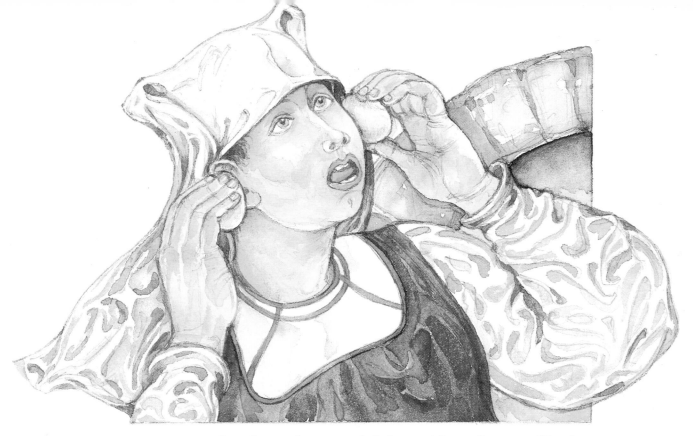

"Now look!" shouted his wife. She pulled and pulled on the eggs. But they would not come off.

Then the man pulled and pulled. But the eggs would not come off.

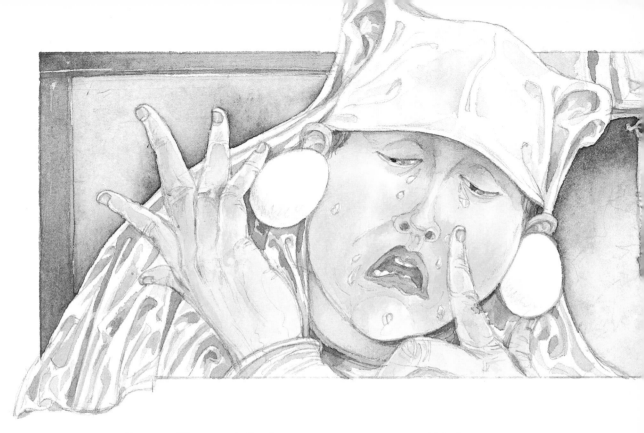

"Oh well," said the man. "We still have one more wish. What shall we choose? Shall we wish for gold coins?"

The woman started to cry. "How can I live with eggs stuck to my ears? All the riches in the world will not make me happy until these eggs are gone."

Well, what could the man do? He had only one wish left. "I wish those eggs were gone," he said.

And in the wink of an eye, the eggs
were gone.

The man and his wife sat down to eat. They talked about all the things they might have wished for.

"We should have wished for two houses," said the man.

"Oh, no," said the woman. "That would be silly. We should have wished for a horse and cart."

"A horse and cart?" said the man. "That
would be silly. Horses need to eat!"

They talked and talked. Then they both
thought of the same wish . . .

they should have wished for three more
wishes!